SOME T
THINKING

Philosophy at Five Miles Per Hour

Jonathan Finch

University Press of America,® Inc.
Lanham · New York · Oxford

Copyright © 2002 by
University Press of America,® Inc.
4720 Boston Way
Lanham, Maryland 20706
UPA Acquisitions Department (301) 459-3366

12 Hid's Copse Rd.
Cumnor Hill, Oxford OX2 9JJ

Library of Congress Cataloging-in-Publication Data

Finch, Jonathan Andrew.
Some thoughts on thinking : philosophy at five miles per hour /
Jonathan Finch.
p. cm
Includes bibliographical references and index.
1. Thought and thinking. 2. Belief and doubt. 3. Philosophy. I. Title.

B105.T54 F56 2002
121—dc21   2002020298 CIP

ISBN 0-7618-2315-8 (paperback : alk. ppr.)

♾™ The paper used in this publication meets the minimum
requirements of American National Standard for Information
Sciences—Permanence of Paper for Printed Library Materials,
ANSI Z39.48—1984

*To my parents, friends, teachers
and students, but most of all
to Hortense Donnan,
a woman of infinite kindness
who showed her grandson the
magical world of books.*

CONTENTS

PART II
NON-ARBITRARY BELIEFS

PART II
A FEW FINAL THOUGHTS

PREFACE

What is thinking about thinking? It is to study the criteria by which recommendable beliefs might be sorted from problematic beliefs. It is to focus on the process of belief justification as opposed to focusing on this or that particular belief.

This book is divided into three sections. The first section discusses some of the similarities and differences between science, theology, philosophy and religion. The second looks at a possible means of sorting arbitrary beliefs from non-arbitrary beliefs. The final section examines some of the concerns raised by the middle section of the work. Stories and tales have been liberally inter-mixed with the discussions mentioned above in an effort to create a text that is extremely readable and yet still philosophical. No previous exposure to philosophy is assumed and the language is free of complex terms.

Jonathan Finch

ACKNOWLEDGMENTS

In both content and style this work owes a very heavy debt to the thought and publications of Susan Haack. Anyone familiar with her work will notice a great deal of influence. James Swindler, both in relation to this work and far beyond it, has provided first class instruction, commentary and advice. The impetus behind the impetus of this work clearly belongs to him. Mark Neunder has readily provided invaluable reviews on many occasions and cannot be thanked enough for his efforts.

The first section of this text and a number of the later chapters were especially improved by the comments and evaluations of Eric Stocks, Marta Plášilová, Greg Thomas and Chris Gajewski, in addition to many of my friends and students, have also contributed some very helpful suggestions. My parents, David and Lucy Finch, have shown a warrior's resolve in tolerating and assisting one caught in the trials and tribulations of philosophy.

My mother also deserves special thanks for her editorial work and critical thought on both early and later versions of this manuscript. Linda Kaufman is also owed a big "thank you" for an outstanding proofread of most of the following material. My sister, Lucy Finch, has graciously assisted with the table of contents. Susan Peabody deserves a great deal of thinks for her camera-ready work on the final draft of this document, and Ibex Index, is to be thanked for putting the index together on such short notice.

The final determination, of course, on the arrangement of the work is mine and I must therefore accept responsibility for its mistakes and imperfections.

PART I

FOUNDATIONS, THINKERS AND THE TOTALITY

CHAPTER 1

THE NORSE GODS, NON-ARBITRARY BELIEFS AND THE TRUTH ABOUT EARTHQUAKES

Odin, Loki and Earthquakes

Among the legends told by the Norse, elder inhabitants of Scandinavia, was the story of Loki and how his imprudence resulted in the quaking of the earth. It is a good story but it first requires a little background.

Odin, also known as the All-Father and the god of war, was the chief of the Norse gods. Thor, the god of thunder and weather, was very popular for he was thought to take a special interest in the affairs of mankind. Thor was also well known for his battles and struggles with the giants of Jotunheim, the enemies of both the gods and humanity.

One of the more infamous dieties was Loki, the Norse god of mischief and strife. At times Loki could be a daring and inventive practical joker and in this capacity he acted as the god of mischief. There was also a darker and very dangerous side to Loki that his charm and cunning could not always hide. At these times Loki acted as the god of strife.

Despite the fact that Loki caused trouble for god and man alike he was tolerated for the other deities, most notably Odin, had occasional need of his subtle and clever mind. Eventually, however, Loki's methods and manners resulted in intolerable offences being given to Thor, his wife the Lady Sif, and the other gods and goddesses. As a consequence of his misbehavior Loki was seized and bound to a rock.

After binding Loki to a rock Odin placed a poisonous serpent over Loki's face, its fangs dripping venom on the trapped god. In this capacity Loki was left to await the end of the world. Despite the fact that he was deserted by all the other gods and goddesses Loki's wife, the goddess Sigryn, remained. Sigryn sat by her husband's side with a large bowl with which she caught the dripping poison.

This was only a partial solution, however, to some of Loki's difficulties. When the bowl eventually filled, as it had to, Sigryn was forced to empty it and for these few moments Loki lay exposed to the serpent's venom. Left unprotected from the terrible poison Loki would struggle violently against his bonds. In fact, so mighty were his attempts to free himself that Loki caused the whole earth to shake. Thus the source of earthquakes, if you were to ask a Norseman, was Loki's wife Sigryn emptying her bowl and Loki's ensuing struggles. Quite a clever explanation, all things considered.

Myth: Some Considerations

The Norse understood their surroundings to be, in part, the product of the lives and actions of human-like divinities. The coming of spring, earthquakes and thunderbolts were thought to have been produced by super human actors and terrible monsters. While super humans fighting with gigantic creatures is both entertaining and easily understood these types of cosmic descriptions can have additional consequences. If human-like actors are thought to move the universe it might become possible to solve some of our problems through communicating with these superhumans. If, on the other hand, the universe is not guided by conscious actors, then these attempts at cosmic communication might prove to be ineffective solutions to our difficulties.

What we believe and why we believe is often times significantly inter-twined with the decisions we make and how we choose to live our lives. What we believe and why we believe would therefore seem to be no small matter.

The aim of this effort is thus an attempt to *think about thinking;* it is an attempt to provide some criteria by which one might start sorting non-arbitrary beliefs from arbitrary beliefs. The text will procede in much the same fashion as this chapter; stories and tales will be used to supplement the discussion of philosophical thought. Taking a moment, however, and beginning a discussion with some terms that are familiar to the student is almost always a good idea. With this in mind I would like to take a moment and briefly discuss some of the similarities and differences between scientific, theological, religious and philosophical beliefs.

CHAPTER 2

AN AMERICAN PHILOSOPHER AND SOME ADVANTAGES OF SCIENCE

Charles Peirce

Charles Peirce was an American thinker who lived and worked in the last half of the nineteenth century and the early part of the twentieth century. In his article "The Fixation of Belief" Peirce attempts to evaluate critically some alternative methods by which we could decide what to think and believe. After pausing to consider some of Peirce's thoughts on this matter we will return to our discussion of philosophy, theology, science and religion.

The "Fixing of Belief"

The first method of determining what to believe, of fixing belief, that Peirce discusses in his paper is the method of *tenacity*. The second method considered is the method of *authority* and the final method evaluated is the method of *science*. Peirce discusses a fourth method, in addition to those mentioned above, but our purposes will be served if we limit our focus to these three.

The method of *tenacity* is simply choosing a belief and sticking to it irrespective of all other concerns. A belief is justified and acceptable if one merely chooses to believe it. As Peirce states "This simple and direct method is really pursued by many men" and "Nor can it be denied that a steady and immovable faith yields great peace of mind."

One difficulty with employing this manner of settling on what to believe is that any belief, no matter how odd or strange, can be selected. Thus one could simply decide to take any belief, that the earth is flat for instance, and thereby settle one's opinion on this matter. As the only criteria for accepting a belief is the finding and securing of a belief, any belief, no matter what the belief, can be fixed in the mind.

Another problem for this method of fixing belief is, as Peirce says, "The social impulse is against it." Individuals in almost every society cannot help but be influenced by the people around them. It is a social reality, argues Peirce, that other people influence how we think and what we believe. The method of *tenacity* is thus not an effective method for settling or fixing beliefs in a social setting.

The second method for fixing belief given by Peirce is the method of *authority*. Under this method of settling belief the government, the church, or some other public institution dictates and controls what is to be believed. To insure that persons do not hold private opinions contrary to the official position these belief officials have the power needed to search out and punish those who fail to think as they are instructed.

This method, while more effective than the method of *tenacity*, is nonetheless rejected by Peirce. The method of *authority* has a weakness and this weakness is that in every society there are individuals who will come to see the method of *authority* as imperfect. Realizing that there is no permanent authority to the state's official beliefs these individuals will, at least in their own minds, question the state's doctrines. Since belief, for Peirce, is not fixed if it is questioned in private, the method of *authority* fails as method of fixing belief.

Peirce, in the following, is now ready to propose his own solution to this problem.

To satisfy our doubts, therefore, it is necessary that a method should be found by which our beliefs may be caused by nothing human, but by some external permanency—by something upon which our thinking has no effect. Some mystics imagine that they have such a method in a private inspiration from on high. But that is only a form of the method of tenacity, in which the conception of truth as something public is not yet developed. Our external permanency would not be external, in our sense, if it was restricted in its influence to one individual. It must be something which affects, or might affect, every man. And, though these affections are necessarily as various as are individual conditions, yet the method must be such that the ultimate conclusion of every man shall be the same, or would be the same if inquiry were sufficiently persisted in. Such is the method of science. Its fundamental hypothesis, restated in more familiar language, is this: There are real things, whose characters are entirely independent of our opinions about them; those realities affect our senses according to regular laws, and, though our sensations are as different as our relations to the objects, yet, by taking advantage of the laws of perception, we can ascertain by reasoning how things really and truly are, and any man, if he have sufficient experience and reason enough about it, will be lead to the one true conclusion....

Unlike the other two methods, the method of *science* relies upon the publicly observable world to validate or invalidate our beliefs. That is, instead of sticking our heads in the sand, as per the method of *tenacity*, or allowing others to decide what we must believe, as per the method of *authority*, the method *science* places the basis for our belief systems outside of human desires and in that which we perceive. For Peirce, then, the preferable method of settling our beliefs about the world is to investigate the world in a observable, repeatable and publicly verifiable manner. In this way Pierce believes our understanding of the world will ultimately, but not necessarily smoothly, make real and lasting advancements.

CHAPTER 3

PHILOSOPHY, SCIENCE AND THE TOTALITY

The problem for science is: What is this substance that
endures when it has ceased to yield us sensations? I
have under my eyes what I call a sheet of paper. What
I actually see is a white area with black marks. When I
touch it, I feel the resistance of a smooth surface, and I
can trace with my finger its rectangular shape. These
sensations are my only assurance that something is
there, outside me. If I turn my eyes in another direction,
the whiteness and the black marks disappear. I have
only the tactile sensations of the resistance of the
smooth rectangular surface. If I lift my finger, these
sensations also disappear. Yet I am absolutely certain
that something is still there—a substance which does
not depend upon my having sensations derived from it.

— F.M. Cornford *Before and After Socrates*

Science: Some Strengths

In the last chapter Peirce recommended science and the
scientific method because of its commitment, at least in theory, to
repeatable and publicly verifiable observations. In this
understanding of science a scientific claim is justified if repeatable
observations can confirm the claim and a scientific claim is not

justified if it cannot be validated by repeated observations. Science is thus, in many respects, more a method of drawing inferences from repeatable and confirmable observations than it is a set system of beliefs.

Science: A Weakness

One of science's greatest strengths, its commitment to the observable is also, in some respects, a substantive weakness. Unless every aspect of existence and reality is, in one way or another, ultimately subject to repeatable and confirmable observational study, then science, by definition of its methods, will never be more than an incomplete study of the totality. It is difficult to see how an investigative method committed to repeatable and confirmable observation could, with any consistency, discuss anything that is not subject to this procedure. Science is thus seemingly forced to be silent about everything that is not observable in repeatable and confirmable manner.

Science, Philosophy and the Totality

The above, of course, is not to assert that science is an ill-conceived, ill-advised or mistaken project. Instead what is intended is that the reader takes away a method of distinguishing philosophy from science. Science is the study of the repeated and confirmable observations and philosophy is the study of science as well as the study of everything else.

Philosophy, given the above, is thus the study of the totality and science, being part of this totality, is part of the study of philosophy. Science, in fact, used to go under the name of natural philosophy and in this dress its derivation from (and dependence upon) philosophy proper was terminologically more apparent. Philosophy is thus the investigation that attempts to combine, account for and explain all of the bits of information yielded to us via our existence. Science, given the above, is the branch of philosophy that is assigned to investigate the repeatable and confirmable observations and while these investigations are important, these investigations are not necessarily the whole or final story.

CHAPTER 4

PHILOSOPHY, THEOLOGY, RELIGION AND BERTRAND RUSSELL

I shall not start with any definition of religion. Religion,
like poetry and most other living things, cannot be
defined. But one may perhaps give some description of
it, or at least some characteristic marks.

— Gilbert Murray, *Five Stages of Greek Religion*

Foundations: Divine, Self-Evident and Assumed

One method of distinguishing philosophy, religion and
theology is to examine each in terms of the manners in which they
form and attempt to justify their respective beliefs. While all three
of these approaches attempt to render accounts of the human
experience they differ in the manners by which they derive and
fashion their belief systems. Philosophers use the term
'epistemology' to designate, among other things, methods of belief
justification. Or, all of this is to say, one can discuss the
similarities and differences between philosophy, theology and
religion in terms of their respective epistemologies.

Before beginning the above, however, it should prove useful to
spend a moment and distinguish between self-evident foundations,

divine foundations and assumed foundations. A foundation, for the purposes of this work, is a starting point in thought; it is a description of the beginnings of belief.

Three Types of Foundations

A Self-Evident Foundation is a thought, idea or belief that once understood, because of its self-evident nature, is thought to be true.

A Divine Foundation is a thought, idea or belief asserting the self-evidence of some aspect of divinity.

An Assumed Foundation is a belief, thought or idea that is uncritically accepted as true.

Defining Theology, Religion and Philosophy

Religion, for purposes of this work, will be defined as systems of thought that employ at least one assumed foundation in the formation of their belief systems. Theologies will be defined as sets of beliefs referencing at least one divine foundation but rejecting the use of assumed foundations. Philosophies are systems of thought that reject the use of assumed and divine foundations and are extremely suspicious of anything claiming to be a self-evident foundation. While the above broad definitions will be supplemented below it should prove useful to first turn to an example.

Bertrand Russell

The following material is drawn from the essay "A Free Man's Worship" which was published by Bertrand Russell in 1903. Russell was a twentieth century British philosopher and Nobel Peace Prize winner.

God, Man and Worship; Another Point of View

The endless praises of the choirs of angels had begun to grow wearisome; for, after all, did he not deserve their praise? Had he not given them endless joy? Would it not be more amusing to obtain undeserved praise, to be worshiped by beings whom he tortured? He smiled inwardly, and resolved that the great drama should be preformed.

For countless ages the hot nebula whirled aimlessly through space. At length it began to take shape, the central mass threw off planets, the planets cooled, boiling seas and burning mountains heaved and tossed, from black masses of cloud hot sheets of rain deluged the barely solid crust. And now the first germ of life grew in the depths of the ocean, and developed rapidly in the fructifying warmth into vast forest trees, huge ferns springing from the damp mould, sea monsters breeding, fighting, devouring, and passing away. And from the monsters, as the play unfolded itself, Man was born, with the power of thought, the knowledge of good and evil and the cruel thirst for worship. And Man saw that all is passing in this mad, monstrous world, that all is struggling to snatch, at any cost, a few brief moments of life before Death's inexorable decree. And Man said: 'There is a hidden purpose, could we but fathom it, and the purpose is good; for we must reverence something, and in the visible world there is nothing worthy of reverence.' And Man stood aside from the struggle, resolving that God had intended harmony to come out of chaos by human efforts. And when he followed the instincts which God had transmitted to him from his ancestry of beasts of prey, he called it Sin, and asked God to forgive him. But he doubted whether he could be justly forgiven, until he invented a divine Plan by which God's wrath was to have been appeased. And seeing the present was bad, he made it yet worse, that thereby the future might be better. And he gave God thanks for the strength that enabled him to forgo even the joys that were possible. And God smiled; and when he saw that Man had become perfect in renunciation and worship, he sent another sun through the sky, which crashed into Man's sun; and all returned again to the nebula.

'Yes,' he murmured, 'it was a good play; I will have it performed again.'

In this chapter it is not what is believed that is at issue; it is why something is believed that is at issue. In the language of this work the above point of view would be classified as a religion, a philosophy or a theology depending on how the above description of reality was justified and demonstrated.

If, for example, this narrative by Bertrand Russell were uncritically assumed to be true this type of belief would be religious belief. If it were derived from at least one divine foundation, without the use of any assumptions, it would be a theology and if it is demonstrated without assumed or a divine foundations it would be a philosophy. Thus the difference between philosophy, theology and religion, in terms of epistemology, is not what is believed; it is why something is believed. Or, in other words, a religious individual, a theologian and a philosopher might all believe the same thing; they differ in regard to the reasons why they hold these same beliefs.

Some Different Conceptions of Philosophy

Philosophy (in General): Philosophy is a study of the totality that does not accept assumed foundations, it does not accept divine foundations and is enormously suspicious of any and all things claiming to be self-evident foundations. Some philosophers will not allow foundations to play any role in their theories of belief justification.

The Foundationless Philosopher: Given the above I would like to define a foundationless philosopher as a thinker who rejects the use of any type of foundation. For the foundationless philosopher foundations are an inappropriate method of constructing belief systems. The feasibility of building a philosophy without the reference to at least one foundation is an issue that must be left to another time.

The Foundational Philosopher: A foundational philosopher is a thinker who references one self-evident foundation and only one self-evident foundation in the construction of his/her beliefs. Assumptions have no place in a foundational philosophy.

The Multiple Foundational Philosopher: Some systems of philosophical thought will appeal to multiple self-evident foundations in their attempts to construct their beliefs. All assumed and divine foundations are excluded from multiple foundational philosophies just as they are excluded from all the previously mentioned conceptions of philosophy.

Some Different Conceptions of Theology

Theology, if we trace the word back far enough, means ' to speak of god' or 'the study of the divine.' It does not, therefore, seem out of line to define theology in terms of an attempt to study, or give an account of, the divine. The philosopher, in the terms of this work, is thus different from the theologian in that the philosopher is not necessarily committed to belief in the supernatural.

It should be noted that some philosophers have attempted to demonstrate the aspects of the divine and it is thus necessary to distinguish what might be termed philosophical theology from theological theology. If a thinker begins either with only self-evident foundations, or with no foundations at all, and the thinker derives the divine, or aspects of the divine, then I would term this thinker a philosophical theologian. While it is the case that the thinker in question studies the divine and is thus, in some sense of the term, a theologian it is also the case that this same thinker did not construct his/her beliefs in the divine from a divine foundation. Since the study of the divine is not mandated by the foundational structure of the thinker's belief system I would consider the thinker to be a philosopher.

Theological theologians, on the other hand, are thinkers who build the divine into their initial foundational structure. Thus while neither the philosophical theologian or the theological theologian knowingly traffics in assumptions the difference between the two can be found in their use of different kinds of foundations.

Theology (in General): Theology is a study of the totality combined with the study of the divine. Theologians are nonetheless different from philosophers in that they, given the preceding distinctions, are thinkers who accept at least one divine foundation. Theologians do not accept assumed foundations.

The Foundational Theologian: The foundational theologian is a thinker who builds a belief system off a single divine foundation. The foundational theologian rejects any and all assumptions.

The Multiple-Foundational Theologian: Multiple foundational theologians appeal to at least one divine foundation and at least one more foundation, divine or self-evident, in their construction of their views of the totality. This type of thinker rejects the use of assumptions, as do all types of theology.

Some Different Conceptions of Religion

Religion (in General): Religion is a study of the totality that employs assumed foundations; it is to form blind beliefs about our experiences.

Limited Religion: Limited religions minimize the use of assumed foundations in the construction of their belief systems. Self-evident and divine foundations may or may not be part of limited religions.

Religious Religion: The term 'Religious Religion' refers to belief systems that regularly appeal to assumptions in justifying and constructing their accounts of the totality. The two other types of foundations may or may not be part of these sets of beliefs.

Science, a Theology, a Religion or a Philosophy?

It might prove useful to stop for a moment and discuss science in terms of the above system of classification. Science is not magical in its operations; science supposedly relies upon repeatable observations to draw its conclusions. Science, thus, relies upon a methodology. If it is uncritically assumed that the scientific methodology yields information about reality then this understanding of science is, in the language of this work, a form of religion. If the scientific method can be shown to derive from a self-evident foundation(s), or from no foundations at all, then this understanding of the scientific method becomes a philosophical understanding. If the scientific method is thought to derive from one or more divine foundations then science becomes a type of theology.

That science must either assume the accuracy of its methodology or provide a demonstration of the reliability of its methods seems fairly clear. To ignore the issue of whether or not evidence can be summoned to support a given investigative procedure and to still think this procedure reliable is to make an assumption; it is an unconscious assumption perhaps, but an assumption nonetheless.

At the risk of being over complete let's consider an example. Imagine we have three people Catherine, Larry and Isabelle who are each scientists and each believe that the scientific method, if used correctly, can yield reasonably reliable results. Catherine, if queried on the matter, cannot provide any justification for her belief in the reliability of the scientific method. She simply assumes that if it is used correctly then it is reliable. Catherine, in this example and in the language of this work, has a religious understanding of the scientific method.

Both Larry and Isabelle, on the other hand, derive their belief in the reliability of scientific method from the other types of foundations. Larry derives his belief in the scientific method from a single divine foundation and thus has theological understanding of science. Isabelle derives her belief from a self-evident foundation and thus has a philosophical understanding of science. All three believe in the reliability of the scientific method; they differ in the reasons why they think the scientific method reliable.

CHAPTER 5

THE BUDDHA, POISONED ARROWS AND THE FOUR NOBLE TRUTHS

It is as if a man had been wounded by an arrow thickly smeared with poison, and his friends and kinsmen were to get a surgeon to heal him, and he were to say, I will not have this arrow pulled out until I know by what man I was wounded...I will not have this arrow pulled out until I know...whether he is tall, or short, or of middle height; or whether he is black, or dark, or yellowish, or whether he comes from such and such a village....

Similarly, it is not on the view that the world is eternal, that it is finite, that body and soul are distinct, or that the Buddha exists after death, that a religious life depends. Whether these views or their opposites are held, there is still rebirth, there is old age, there is death, and grief, lamentation, suffering, sorrow and despair...I have not spoken to these views because they do not conduce to absence of passion, or to tranquility and Nirvana.

And what have I explained? Suffering have I explained, the cause of suffering, the destruction of suffering, and the path that leads to the destruction of suffering have I explained. For this is useful"

— The Buddha

The Buddha

The word Buddha derives from the Sanskrit term, *budh*, which means both 'to wake up' and 'to know.' The Buddha is thus, 'The Awakened One' or 'The Enlightened One.' According to legend the Buddha draws his name from an answer he gave to a question, but first a little background.

It seems that from time to time it is possible, if one is in the right place at the right time, to meet individuals capable of making the burdens of humanity lighter. The Buddha, according to the tales, is one such individual. In fact, as some legends have it, ordinary folk who came into contact with the Buddha began to wonder aloud whether or not Buddha was divine. When this question of divinity was put to the Buddha himself he denied any super-natural status and, instead, described himself as simply one who is awake. Thus, as this story is told, the Buddha's name comes in answer to a question of self-description.

While it seems that many would have believed the Buddha if he had said he was divine —indeed a good number of present day Buddhists consider the Buddha to be divine—the Buddha, according to this story, did not take this route. Instead the Buddha answers the question of his own divinity with the extraordinarily powerful— No, I am not a divine, but I am awake. Or, in other words, I, Buddha, am just like you, and you are just like the Buddha. The difference between you and the Buddha is that the Buddha is awake and you are not yet awake.

A Quick Disclaimer

It is important to note that the above description of the Buddha and Buddhism, while within one school of Buddhist thought, is outside of the tradition and beliefs of another very popular interpretation of the Buddha and his message. This school of thought believes, among other things, that the Buddha was in fact divine and that one can pray to the Buddha. This belief in the divinity of the Buddha exists despite some reported claims to the contrary by the Buddha himself, but we need not debate these concerns here and now. All that it is necessary to note is that the understanding of the Buddha presented in this chapter is disputed.

The Four Noble Truths

Upon achieving enlightenment the Buddha gave his first lecture on The Four Noble Truths. These four truths provide, in the terms of this work, the foundations of Buddhism. Pausing a moment and taking a look at these foundations should provide us with a good example of what is meant by the term foundation, or starting point, in thought.

The first noble truth, or the first foundation of Buddhism, is that all of life is *dukkha*. *Dukkha* is a word that can be translated as suffering, but this is too simplistic a rendering. *Dukkha* implies suffering but it also has other implications as well. *Dukkha*, in this context, is better understood to mean that life lived counter to nature is painful and that if we want to rid ourselves of this suffering we need to live in harmony with nature. We suffer because we don't understand how to live with our surroundings and ourselves.

The Second Noble Truth states that life is painful and problematic because most of us are fighting with nature when we crave individualistic satisfaction. For the Buddha all of existence and reality is ultimately one; it is a unified whole. Since any attempts to live an individuated existence ultimately runs counter to this unity, individualistic desires cause pain. To be released from pain we have to learn to renounce the desires that cause us to fight and act counter to the oneness of nature; this is the Second Noble Truth.

The Third Noble Truth follows logically from the Second. If the cause of life's dislocation (*dukkha*) is selfish craving, its cure lies in the over-coming of such craving. If we could be released from the narrow limits of self-interest into the vast expanse of universal life, we would be relieved of our torment. The Fourth

Noble Truth prescribes how the cure can be accomplished. The overcoming of *tanha* (selfish craving), the way out of our captivity, is through the Eightfold Path...."

— Huston Smith *The World's Religions*

The Eightfold Path

1. Right views.
2. Right aspiration.
3. Right speech.
4. Right conduct.
5. Right effort.
6. Right mindfulness.
7. Right contemplation.
8. Right livelihood.

This, of course, is a great opportunity to jump into a deeper discussion of the eightfold path and Buddhism in general but this would take us too far from our current purposes and must be left to another time. The above discussion has I hope provided a good example of a system of thought that can be understood in terms of foundations. In addition to providing a quick introduction to some of the Buddha's thought, the four noble truths also provide an example of how, from a very few basic ideas, a whole way of life can be constructed.

Foundational Thought: A Consideration

Something to note about foundations is that 'as go the foundations so goes the thought built upon those foundations.' While foundations are a powerful method of creating a system of beliefs they also contain an Achilles Heel, a critical weakness. If a foundation can be shown to be problematic, beliefs that have been influenced by reference to that foundation will, in all likelihood, need some re-thinking. A foundational system of thought can thus be substantively weakened and sometimes completely under-mined if one of its foundations proves to be erroneous.

CHAPTER 6

DIVINE FOUNDATIONS AND
A NECESSARY GOD?

A Divine Foundation?

A good example of a possible divine foundation can be found in the writings of Saint Anselm, an 11th century theologian. Anselm combines, what I have termed, a divine foundation with a self-evident foundation to reach his conclusion that God exists. The content of these foundations, however, is a little complex and thus we will try to move through them slowly.

The first foundation, the divine foundation, begins with the idea that God is the greatest possible being and that there is no being greater than God. Nothing exists that is greater than God and God is the greatest thing that exists.

The second foundation, the self-evident foundation, maintains that necessary existence is greater than possible existence. That which must exist is greater than that which might only exist.

When these two foundations are combined we supposedly derive the conclusion that God exists and that God exists necessarily. If God's existence were not necessary there would be a being greater than God and this possibility is excluded by the first foundation. God's existence is thus mandated by his own greatness.

If the above seems a little confusing this should not overly trouble the reader. This and similar demonstrations of divine existence have long been the subject of great dispute and enormous controversy. This is not the place, however, for a sustained analysis of this discussion. The above should serve, nonetheless, as an example of what is intended by the term 'a divine foundation.'

Something to Note

There is an interesting inter-play between the two foundations that is worth mentioning. The first foundation in conjunction with the second foundation yields a conclusion that is not explicitly contained in either foundation considered in isolation. The conclusion, one might say, is a synthesis of the two foundations; the inter-play between the two thoughts yields a third thought. More will be said on this in coming chapters but it is worthwhile to take a moment and get a feel for how foundations and beliefs can work together to justify further beliefs.

PART II

NON-ARBITRARY BELIEFS

A Philosophical Account of
Belief Recommendation

The first section of this book compared, contrasted and offered definitions of philosophy, science, theology and religion. The work now moves on to examine some of the concerns one might encounter in, and how one might go about, constructing a philosophical theory of belief recommendation. A format similar to the preceding will be followed; stories and tales will be used to help explain the thoughts under discussion.

CHAPTER 7

PERSONAL FINANCE, APPEARANCE AND REALITY

The origin of things, if things have an origin, cannot be revealed to me, if revealed at all, until I have traveled very far from it, and many revolutions of the sun must precede my first dawn. The light as it appears hides the candle. Perhaps there is no source of things at all, no simpler form from which things evolved, but only an endless succession of different complexities. In that case nothing would be lost by joining the procession wherever one happens to come upon it, and following it as long as one's legs hold out. Every one might still observe a typical bit of it; he would not have understood anything better if he had seen more things; he would only have had more to explain."

— George Santayana, *Skepticism and Animal Faith*

Money

The following is drawn from Shel Silverstein's masterful work of poetry and sketch, *Where the Sidewalk Ends*.

Smart

My dad gave me one dollar bill
'Cause I'm his smartest son,
And I swapped it for two shiny quarters
'Cause two is more than one!

And then I took the quarters
And traded them to Lou
For three dimes–I guess he don't know
That three is more than two!

Just then, along came old blind Bates
And just 'cause he can't see
He gave me four nickels for my three dimes,
And four is more than three!

And I took the nickels to Hiram Coombs
Down at the seed-feed store,
And the fool gave me five pennies for them,
And five is more than four!

And then I went and showed my dad,
And he got red in the cheeks
And closed his eyes and shook his head–
Too proud of me to speak!

The above might be said to demonstrate, among other things, some of the differences between appearance and reality. When it comes to coins and mediums of exchange quantity is not always quality; more is not always better. As the poem suggests dad's smartest son should have been a little more careful in his dealings with the local currency market.

The difficulty in distinguishing between appearance and reality, however, would not seem to be limited to matters of trade and barter. Attempting to form beliefs about ourselves and that which seems to surround us can prove to be a very tricky matter. Not everything is as it appears and without a reliable means of telling the difference between appearance and reality it would seem hard to avoid a great deal of doubt and uncertainty.

The doubting of everything, or nearly everything, has been termed in philosophy the practice of skepticism. To be a skeptic is to suspend belief in nearly everything. Some skeptics, in fact, claim to suspend belief in everything.

To commit one's self to a belief is, for a philosopher, to have a reason for the holding of this belief. If it is not possible to tell the difference between appearance and reality then the philosophically minded would seem to lack a criteria by which to determine what is real and what is illusion. Without criteria for deciphering our experiences, without criteria by which appearance can be separated from reality, the formation of a non-arbitrary belief about our experiences would seem nearly impossible.

Or, that is to say, one cannot simply assume, at least if one wants to be a philosopher, that our senses, thoughts or perceptions represent the totality in an accurate manner. One of the jobs of the philosopher, therefore, is to provide, if possible, an account of how one forms non-arbitrary beliefs about our experiences. One method of providing such an account is to begin with radical doubt, the doubting of everything that can be doubted, and then attempting to reconstruct our beliefs upon foundations solid enough to withstand this process of radical doubt.

A good example of the application of this process can be found in the work of Rene Descartes, a famous seventeenth century French thinker. The next chapter will discuss some of Descartes' thoughts on radical doubt and part of Descartes' solution to this problem.

CHAPTER 8

THE THINKER, THE SKEPTIC AND A FRENCH PHILOSOPHER

Skepticism: 1. A state of doubting. 2. A state of suspension of judgment. 3. A state of unbelief or non-belief. Skepticism ranges from complete, total disbelief in everything, to a tentative doubt in the process of reaching certainty.

— Peter Angeles, *Dictionary of Philosophy*

The Thinker and the Skeptic

One of the great difficulties facing anyone who would attempt a philosophical account of the human experience is the challenge posed by the skeptic. To claim that the reality is "this way and not that way" is to make an assertion. Whenever a claim is advanced, whenever it is stated that "(x) is justified and (y) is not justified" the skeptic can ask, "How do you know that (x) is justified and (y) is not justified?" The skeptic challenges the thinker to give an explanation, in the form of a reasoned and evidential demonstration, of why he or she thinks any given thought is a recommendable representation of reality.

The remainder of this work is an attempt to provide and discuss an answer to the skeptic; it is an attempt to provide a means by which the formation and justification of non-arbitrary beliefs seems possible. It should be noted that the process of belief justification to be discussed derives directly from the work and thought of Susan Haack. Anyone wishing a more detailed discussion of this material should take a look at the chapter notes provided at the end of the text. It is hoped that, among other things, this work will provide a springboard into Haack's invaluable publications.

Two modern philosophers have articulated the skeptical challenge in such a way as to significantly influence modern and contemporary philosophy. While there are many versions of this challenge our purposes will be served if we examine the form it takes in the writings of Rene Descartes and Immanuel Kant. Descartes, a seventeenth century French thinker, predates and influences Kant, an eighteenth century German thinker, and thus it is probably best to start our discussion of skepticism with Descartes.

Descartes and Skepticism

Descartes opens one of his more famous works with a bit of autobiography that quickly leads into a discussion regarding the difficulties he encountered in attempting to fashion an accurate set of beliefs. In the following the desire for certainty drives Descartes to question everything that he can question. By calling every belief that can be doubted into doubt, Descartes hopes to create an intellectual filter which, if handled properly, will sort truth from falsehood in an infallible manner.

> Some years ago I was struck by the large number of falsehoods that I had accepted as true in my childhood, and by the highly doubtful nature of the whole edifice that I had subsequently based on them. I realized that it was necessary, once in the course of my life, to demolish everything completely and start again right from the foundations if I wanted to establish anything...that was stable and likely to last....

Reason now leads me to think that I should hold back my assent from opinions which are not completely certain and indubitable just as carefully as I do from those which are patently false. So, for the purpose of rejecting all my opinions, it will be enough if I find in each of them at least some reason for doubt. And to do this I will not need to run through them all individually, which would be an endless task. Once the foundations of a building are undermined, anything built on them collapses of its own accord; so I will go straight for the basic principles on which all my former beliefs rested....

As I think about this more carefully, I see plainly that there are never any sure signs by means of which being awake can be distinguished from being asleep....

While our apparent inability to distinguish dreams from reality poses a serious obstacle to the construction of legitimate beliefs Descartes is not yet finished out-lining his skeptical challenge. He now moves on to consider what he believes to be an even greater difficulty. It is possible, argues Descartes, that all of our experiences could be the result of some sort of massive illusion. All of our memories, all of our perceptions, all of our experiences might be nothing more than a very cleverly constructed deception.

I will suppose therefore that not God, who is supremely good and the source of truth, but rather some malicious demon of the utmost power and cunning has employed all of his energies in order to deceive me...I shall consider myself as not having hands or eyes, or flesh, or blood or senses, but as falsely believing that I have all these things. I shall stubbornly and firmly persist in this meditation; and, even if it is not in my power to know any truth, I shall at least...guard against assenting to any falsehoods, so that the deceiver, however powerful and cunning he may be, will be unable to impose on me in the slightest degree....

Sometimes referred to as 'the evil demon objection' the above presents a very formidable obstacle to the goal of attaining infallible beliefs. Not only it is apparently impossible to distinguish dreams from reality but the possible plots of a powerful and evil demon makes it even more difficult to distinguish reality from illusion. Things are starting to look rather bleak for Descartes' project of finding and fashioning a set of beliefs that he can be certain is inerrant.

Descartes' Answer to the Skeptic

The value of Descartes' answer to the skeptic is disputed but it is interesting nonetheless to take a look at what he has to say on this matter:

> But I have convinced myself that there is absolutely nothing in the world, no sky, no earth, no minds, no bodies. Does it now follow that I too do not exist? No: if I thought of anything at all then I certainly existed. But there is a deceiver of supreme power and cunning who is deliberately and constantly deceiving me. In that case I too undoubtedly exist, if he is deceiving me; and let him deceive me as much as he can, he will never bring it about that I am nothing so long as I think that I am something. So after considering everything very thoroughly, I must finally conclude that this proposition, *I am, I exist,* is necessarily true whenever it is put forward by me or conceived in my mind....

Descartes, in the above passage, believes that he has found one thing, one thought, one belief, that cannot be doubted. The quest for inerrant belief has led him to the conclusion that he has knowledge of his own existence. While it might be the case that Descartes is systematically and completely deceived about everything he sees, hears, tastes, touches and smells he cannot, according to Descartes, be deceived about his own existence. The very possibility of deception necessities that there must be something which is to be deceived. It is not possible to deceive that which does not exist.

Having achieved certainty in one belief, the belief in his own existence, Descartes now attempts to determine if he can discover any additional certain beliefs.

I am certain that I am a thing which thinks. But if I am indeed certain of this I must know what is requisite to render me certain of anything. I must possess a standard of certainty. In this first knowledge which I have gained, what is there that assures me of its truth? Nothing except the clear and distinct perception of what I state...Accordingly, I can establish as a general rule that all things which I perceive very clearly and very distinctly, are true....

Clear and distinct perception thus becomes Descartes guarantee of the certainty of a thought or belief. The reasoning on this: Descartes is certain of his own existence and this certainty springs, according to Descartes, from the clear and distinct perception of his own existence. The guarantee of his first certain belief was that he clearly and distinctly perceived the need for his own existence. Other certain beliefs will thus, according to Descartes, be guaranteed by clear and distinct perceptions. With this new method in hand Descartes then sets about reconstructing a system of beliefs.

Some Considerations on Descartes' Answer

The value and success of much of what Descartes has to say in his answer to the skeptic depends greatly upon the criteria of clear and distinctness. If clear and distinct impressions fail to guarantee truth then Descartes' answer to the skeptic may become problematic. The reader should keep in mind that it is possible that Descartes has reached his conclusion by a method other than clearness and distinctness and that Descartes has mistaken one method for another. It should also be noted that it is difficult for many to accept that claim that certainty in thought and belief can be achieved by simply referencing the mental appearance of our own thoughts. Clear and distinct experiences, in and of themselves, would not appear to be necessarily true.

Thinking, Knowing and Existing

It appears to me that the strength of Descartes' proof of his own existence hinges upon three things. It hinges upon a self-evident foundation, the self-awareness of a perception and upon a very tight chain of reasoning. One might re-phrase Descartes' proof, in light of the above, as follows:

1. The experience of a perception is only possible if something exists which experiences the perception.

2. I, René Descartes, am currently experiencing a perception.

3. I, Reneé Descartes, must exist.

The above, of course, while a powerful demonstration is not, at the same time, terribly informative. To be aware of one's own perceptions and to therefore be aware of one's own existence, while providing a fine starting point for thought, needs to be substantially supplemented in order to provide a significant counter to skepticism. Descartes is aware of this need for supplementation and attempts to provide this supplement by introducing the criteria of clear and distinct ideas as guarantees of truth. Further discussion of Descartes' thought on this matter, however, would take us too far from our current purposes and must be left to another time. Coming chapters will discuss criteria other than clearness and distinctness by which justified and unjustified beliefs might be distinguished and sorted.

A Foundation and More Skepticism

The next chapter will discuss another version of the skeptical challenge. Dreams and evil demons are not the only things that provide obstacles to philosophy and philosophically constructed beliefs. Nonetheless, before proceeding to these further challenges, it is important to note that Descartes' proof of his own existence may provide a possible foundation for philosophical thought. More will be said on this later but it should be noted that Descartes' "I think therefore I am," is a powerful demonstration of personal existence to any who are aware of their own thoughts.

CHAPTER 9

PARROTS, INVALID KINGS AND A GERMAN PHILOSOPHER

The second skeptical challenge I would like to discuss is a little complicated and thus it might be best to introduce it with a story. With this in mind I would like to borrow a tale from a charming book entitled *A Thousand and One Arabian Nights*.

An Arabian Parrot

For those only passingly familiar with *A Thousand and One Arabian Nights* let me spend a few moments and fill in some of the details. The book opens by describing the problems of King Shahryar and his brother, King Shah Zaman. The brothers shared a difficulty and this shared difficulty was unfaithful wives. One of the brothers, King Shahryar, decides that the only solution to what he perceives as universal female infidelity is to take a different wife each night and have her put to death in the morning.

Over the next three years hundreds of women are put to an ill deserved death. As the death toll grows one of the daughters of the King's chief vizier devises a desperate plan. The vizier's daughter decides to gamble her life on the hope that her extensive education would allow her to fully occupy the King's nightly attention with stories and tales. The delay of sexual intercourse between the King and his new bride would, if the plan worked correctly, forestall, at least for a little while, the King's executions.

Much to the distress of her father this courageous young lady volunteers to be the King's next wife and so begins *A Thousand and One Arabian Nights*. The vizier's daughter, via her story telling, successfully preserves her life and before the end of 'a thousand and one nights' the King decides that he had been hasty in judgment of women and he rescinds his terrible policy.

The following excerpt is drawn from "The Tale of the Husband and the Parrot" which is itself part of a much longer story entitled "The Fisherman and the Jinnee."

There once was a merchant who married a perfectly beautiful wife, who was lovely and graceful. He was, however, so madly jealous of her that he would not leave her to conduct his business. At last an occasion arose that compelled him to travel. So he went to a bird market and bought a parrot for one hundred gold pieces. Then he placed the parrot in his house and expected it to act as a *duenna* and report to him everything that happened during his absence, for the bird was cunning and never forgot what it saw or heard.

Now the merchant's fair wife had fallen in love with a young Turk, who visited her during her husband's absence, and she treated him to a feast during the day and lay with him during the night. Soon the merchant completed his business, returned home, and began at once to question the parrot about the conduct of his wife while he was in foreign countries.

"Your wife has a male friend, who spent every night with her during your absence," the parrot declared.

Thereupon the husband went to his wife in a violent rage and gave her the beating of her life. Afterward, suspecting that one of the slave girls had been tattling to the master, the woman called them together and made them swear to tell the truth. Indeed, they all swore that they had kept her secret, and they revealed to her that the parrot was the one who had squealed, insisting that they had heard it with their own ears.

As a result the woman ordered one of the girls to set a hand mill under the cage and to grind with it. Another girl was commanded to sprinkle water through the cage and roof, and a third to run around flashing a mirror of bright steel throughout the night. Next morning when the husband returned home after being entertained by one of his friends, he ordered that the parrot be brought before him and asked what had taken place while he was away.

"Pardon me, oh master," said the bird, "I could neither hear nor see anything because of the thunder and lightning that lasted throughout the murky night."

Since it happened to be the height of summer, the master was astounded and cried "But we're now in July, and there aren't any storms or rain."

"By Allah," replied the parrot "I saw everything with my own eyes."

Thereupon the merchant, not suspecting his wife's plot, became extremely angry, for he now believed that he had wrongly accused his wife. So he reached out, pulled the parrot from his cage, and dashed it upon the ground with such force that he killed it on the spot....

The story continues and in the end the merchant discovers his wife's trickery and kills both her and her young lover.

Parrots, Rain Storms and Invalid Kings

The parrot, in the preceding story, was deceived into making a false report to his master. The parrot thought that it had perceived a heavy rainstorm but the reality behind its perceptions was in fact quite different. What is perceived and what is real, one might say, can at times be very different things.

Given the above, in the case of the parrot, the merchant and the fake rainstorm, the parrot had accurately reported what it had perceived. While the parrot's report would have appeared to be accurate for anyone in the parrot's cage, the parrot's report was inaccurate for anyone outside of the parrot's cage. The parrot, however, only had access to that which entered the cage. It could not leave the cage to determine if what its senses were reporting was being reported accurately.

Kant, a late 18th century German philosopher, distinguished between the perceived and the unperceived. We have access, as it were, to the former but not the latter. We experience the perceived but we cannot experience the unperceived.

Kant's distinction between the perceived and unperceived can be understood, in part, in terms of the parrot and the cage. That which is outside of the cage is the 'the unperceived,' and that which is inside the cage is 'the perceived.' This point, however, can be a difficult one and at the risk of being over complete I would like to use another example to help demonstrate the issue under discussion. Consider the following story:

> It is around the turn of the century and a doctor of some note has a serving girl working in his home. The girl's tasks include cleaning and maintaining the residence. While performing her duties the girl misses a step on a flight of stairs and takes a terrible fall.
>
> It is the nature of young lady's misfortune that she hits her head such that the top part of her skull is removed and her brain is left exposed to the open air. The girl is still very much alive and feels relatively fine considering the circumstances.
>
> The doctor, for some unknown reason, takes this moment to conduct an experiment. He takes the girl into his office and touches live wires to the exposed parts of her brain. The young lady reports seeing flashes of blue when one part is touched and flashes of red when another part is touched. She dies a few days later.

While this is a tragic story and this doctor, at the very least, has some serious explaining to do, I would like to leave the ethical side of this story alone and focus on another question. Given the above, let us suppose some sort of nutrient bucket could be cooked up such that it supplied a given brain with the essential biological and chemical elements necessary for its survival. Add to this situation an extremely sophisticated computer which is wired to the brain in a manner such that all of the sensory receptors of the brain are under the control of the super computer.

Let's also suppose, by virtue of this arrangement, that this super computer could create sensations and perceptions that were indistinguishable from real ones. Thus, this brain in a bucket, could theoretically live for years and never realize that its perceptions were wholly false and generated by a computer and a deranged surgeon. It would seem in fact that this brain in the bucket could live its entire life and never know it was a brain in a bucket.

The situation facing the brain in the bucket is the same sort of situation facing the parrot in the cage or humanity as it tries to perceive, observe and understand. If we cannot experience the totality directly but must instead rely upon middlemen and messengers we need to be cautious in our attempts at investigation. Just as the invalid king, too sick to inspect the realm, must rely upon his ministers and agents for information about his kingdom, we must rely upon our senses, and not direct inspection, for a good deal of our information about ourselves and our apparent surroundings.

One should note, however, that this proposal for an indirect investigation of the reality is outside of a pure Kantian tradition. For Kant the unperceived lies beyond that which can be known and all that can be said of it is that it is unperceived and nothing more. Kant's solution to his own puzzle is well worth studying but its presentation and consideration would take us too far from our current purposes.

Conclusion

While Kant has presented a very powerful challenge with his division of reality and perception, I think this affair admits of at least a partial solution. The up-coming chapters will discuss this partial solution in some detail. Before concluding this chapter, however, it is also important to note that while some of Kant's ideas have been presented to assist in the formation of the skeptical challenge, Kant himself was not a skeptic.

CHAPTER 10

PUMPKINS, SHADE TREES AND OTHER CONSIDERATIONS IN AGRICULTURE

Some Exciting New Theories in Agriculture

In this chapter we are going to begin considering some responses to the skeptical challenges presented in the last few chapters. But first, and in order to give us an additional frame of reference, I would like to take a moment and look over part of a short story entitled "How I Edited an Agricultural Paper" by the famous humorist Mark Twain. The following tall-tale should provide a good context for our discussion of truth and falsehood later in the chapter.

How I Edited an Agricultural Paper

I did not take temporary editorship of an agricultural paper without misgivings. Neither would a landsman take command of a ship without misgivings. But I was in circumstances that made the salary an object. The regular editor of the paper was going off for a holiday, and I accepted the terms he offered, and took his place.

The sensation of being at work again was luxurious, and I wrought all the week with unflagging pleasure. We went to press, and I waited a day with some solicitude to see whether my effort was going to attract any notice. As I left the office, toward sundown, a group of men and boys at the foot of the stairs dispersed with one impulse, and gave me passageway, and I heard one or two of them say: "That's him!" I was naturally pleased by this incident. The next morning I found a similar group at the foot of the stairs, and scattering couples and individuals standing here and there in the street and over the way, watching me with interest. The group separated and fell back as I approached, and I heard a man say, "Look at his eye!" I pretended not to observe the notice I was attracting, but secretly I was pleased with it, and was purposing to write an account of it to my aunt. I went up the short flight of stairs, and heard cheery voices, and a ringing laugh as I drew near the door, which I opened, and caught a glimpse of two young rural-looking men, whose faces blanched and lengthened when they saw me, and then they both plunged through the window with a great crash. I was surprised.

In about half an hour an old gentleman, with a flowing beard and a fine but rather austere face, entered and sat down at my invitation. He seemed to have something on his mind. He took off his hat and set it on the floor, and got out of it a red silk handkerchief and a copy of our paper.

He put the paper on his lap, and while he polished his spectacles with his handkerchief he said, "Are you the new editor?"

I said I was.

"Have you ever edited an agricultural paper before?"

"No," I said; "this is my first attempt."

"Very likely. Have you had any experience in agriculture practically?"

"No; I believe I have not."

"Some instinct told me so," said the old gentleman, putting on his spectacles, and looking over them at me with asperity, while he folded his paper into a convenient shape. "I wish to read you what must have made me have that instinct. It was this editorial. Listen, and see if it was you that wrote it:

'Turnips should never be pulled, it injures them. It is much better to send a boy up and let him shake the tree.'

"Now, what do you think of that?—for I really suppose you wrote it?"

"Think of it? Why, I think it is good. I think it is sense. I have no doubt that every year millions and millions of bushels of turnips are spoiled in this township alone by being pulled in a half-ripe condition, when, if they had sent a boy up to shake the tree—"

"Shake your grandmother! Turnips don't grow on trees!"

"Oh, they don't, don't they? Well, who said they did? The language was intended to be figurative, wholly figurative. Anybody that knows anything will know that I meant that the boy should shake the vine."

Then this old person got up and tore his paper all into small shreds, and stamped on them, and broke several things with his cane, and said I did not know as much as a cow; and then went out and banged the door after him, and, in short, acted in such a way that I fancied he was displeased about something. But not knowing what the trouble was, I could not be any help to him.

Pretty soon after this a long, cadaverous creature, with lanky locks hanging down to his shoulders, and a week's stubble bristling from the hills and valleys of his face, darted within the door, and halted, motionless, with finger on lip, and head and body bent in listening attitude. No sound was heard. Still he listened. No sound. Then he turned the key in the door, and came elaborately tiptoeing toward me till he was within long reaching distance of me, when he stopped and, after scanning my face with intense interest for a while, drew a folded copy of our paper from his bosom, and said:

"There, you wrote that. Read it to me—quick! Relieve me. I suffer."

I read as follows; and as the sentences fell from my lips I could see the relief come, I could see the drawn muscles relax, and the anxiety go out of the face, and rest and peace steal over the features like the merciful moonlight over a desolate landscape:

Concerning the pumpkin. This berry is a favorite with the natives of the interior of New England who prefer it to the gooseberry for the making of fruit-cake,

> *and who likewise give it the preference over the*
> *raspberry for feeding cows, as being more filling and*
> *fully as satisfying....But the custom of planting it in the*
> *front yard with the shrubbery is fast going out of vogue,*
> ***for it is now generally conceded that the pumpkin as***
> ***shade tree is a failure...***

The excited listener sprang toward me to shake hands, and said: "There, there—that will do. I know I am all right now, because you have read it just as I did, word for word. But, stranger, when I first read it this morning, I said to myself, I never, never believed it before...[but]...My reason has stood the strain of one of your agricultural articles, and I know that nothing can ever unseat it now. Good-by, sir...."

Twain's story continues and ends with a confrontation between the 'new editor' and the old editor who returns from his holiday prematurely to save the reputation of the journal. The rest of the tale is amusing and worth the trouble to find a copy.

Setting the Stage

Twain's use of obviously poor, if not down right impossible, agricultural advice provides a good setting for discussing issues of truth and falsehood. That is, our reason for focusing upon rather mundane issues like harvesting vegetables is that many people can agree about what is good advice and wild nonsense in farming. This type of agreement about what constitutes good and bad thinking is much harder to achieve, for instance, in political, religious or economic arenas. With this in mind, let's turn to examining Twain's short story with the eventual goal of using this examination to provide some possible responses to the division of perception and reality.

The "Truth" about Pumpkins and Turnips

I mentioned earlier that Twain's short story contains poor, if not downright mistaken, agricultural advice. The question that is of interest to us now is the reason why we consider his theories to be mistaken. The seeming answer to this question is that Twain's agricultural recommendations are considered to be silly, if not down right outrageous, because they inaccurately represent the situation.

In light of the above, statements are usually considered to be true if they accurately describe the world and statements are usually considered to be false if they fail to accurately describe the world. Or, the reason why the statement 'an ordinary pumpkin makes a poor shade tree' is true is because an ordinary pumpkin, in reality, is a poor shade tree. While this may seem a little obvious at first it is here that Kant's distinction between the perceived and the unperceived becomes important. The problem that arises with defining truth as 'an accurate description of reality' is that if we cannot access anything beyond our perceptions it would seem very difficult to know when our beliefs accurately, or inaccurately, represent that which is supposedly real.

Kant's point about the distinction between the perceived and the real can thus be a very difficult dichotomy to escape in a philosophical theory of belief justification. If the world is unknowable because we cannot ever get directly at it and our beliefs, to be true or false, have to be understood in terms of accuracy and inaccuracy in describing this unknowable thing, we have a bit of a problem. Unable to access the real we are left with thoughts, ideas and beliefs but apparently with no method by which we can ascertain their veracity.

The above, however, is not to claim that functional and working beliefs cannot be derived from our experiences. It would seem necessary, nonetheless, to understand functional and working beliefs as functional and working beliefs and not as true or final accounts. This new term, this working criterion, needs to be discussed but first I would like to introduce another story. The following is drawn from the thought of the ancient Chinese philosopher Mencius.

Ox Mountain

Mencius, like many Eastern sages, was an expert at using the story or tale to demonstrate his philosophical ideas. To explain some of his ideas about humanity and society Mencius relied upon the story of Ox Mountain. The story in short:

> Ox Mountain was located near a great Chinese city. Ox Mountain's proximity to such a large urban center soon resulted in the mountain being stripped of every available resource. Mines were sunk into its sides and its forests were cut for lumber. Sheep and cattle roamed its slopes stripping away all of its vegetation. The continuous plunder of the mountain robbed it of its' natural beauty. In fact it was not uncommon for those who had never seen Ox Mountain in its original condition to think of the mountain as ugly and unsightly.

Mencius used the story of Ox Mountain to explain some of his views about, what might be termed today, the effects of mass society on human psychology. Humanity, for Mencius, in its natural condition is beautiful, peaceful and kind. If humans seem to be ugly and uncaring it is because living in urban society robs humanity of its natural tendencies towards benevolence. If one were to see humanity before the corrupting influences of massed society went to work on its personality, humanity would appear quite gentle, peaceful and considerate. It is not mankind, therefore, that is bad or cruel; rather it is the influences of crowded living that turns the hearts of people and makes them vicious.

While this tale, at the very least, contains a very interesting hypothesis concerning human nature it is not really feasible to pursue this issue at this moment. The above story is of interest to us, at this point in time, for its ability to help explain the concept of a 'working' belief. By using an example that is not literally true, comparing humanity to a specific mountain, Mencius is able to provide some thoughts on how it might be possible to alleviate some of our suffering. Or, that is to say, if it turned out that Mencius's hypothesis on this matter assisted us in eliminating a good deal of our social troubles we would say that while his story was not literally true it was a workable approximation of reality.

Working Beliefs, an Introduction

A working belief is thus a belief, that while not literally true, is a belief that allows for, and facilitates, the achievement of goals. While beliefs that are inerrant are likely to be preferable to working beliefs certainty may not be a readily achievable standard in human thought. The success of a belief in assisting us in achieving our purposes and desires is thus an imperfect investigative tool. It, however, is also a standard for belief which is subject to testing; one belief can be compared to another in terms of their effectiveness in achieving goals. A working standard of thought, because it is subject to a test and demonstration, thus becomes a non-arbitrary standard for belief justification; at least in regard to some beliefs.

CHAPTER 11

BELIEFS THAT WORK,
MISTAKEN BELIEFS THAT
WORK AND AN OLD IRISH GOD

Working Beliefs

Working beliefs were introduced in the last chapter as rough approximations of reality that assist us in interacting with that which we experience. Working beliefs, once again, are beliefs that while useful in achieving given ends, are also beliefs that are imperfect. Nonetheless, and in spite of their acknowledged difficulties, working beliefs provide a basis by which some beliefs can be compared one to another. Beliefs that allow for a more efficient and effective interaction with our goals and the cosmos are, in terms of a working criterion, beliefs that are preferable to those which are less efficient and less effective. While a working criterion of belief adjudication can judge only between beliefs that are put to efficiency and effectiveness tests, it is nonetheless seemingly possible to accept or reject some beliefs via a reference to these tests.

Limitations on Working Beliefs

One cannot make too much of this point that we should not mistake working beliefs as the ideal of inquiry. Inquiry, at least for many, aims at providing a true and accurate description of all that we can know. For these thinkers attempts to understand investigations and investigating in terms of efficiency and prediction are attempts that are too narrow in focus. Investigation, philosophy, science, theology and religion are not about fashioning working beliefs; they are about fashioning true and accurate beliefs and nothing less than true and accurate beliefs.

The power of the skeptical challenge is really brought out at this point in the discussion. If it is not possible to find a significant number of beliefs that are certain then we may be forced to settle for less than certainty in what we think to be true. The skeptic and the challenges of skepticism thus provide a bit of philosophical water-shed. If one thinks that skepticism fails to undermine certainty in matters of thought then it is likely that one will continue to search for certain beliefs. If, on the other hand, one thinks that skepticism has raised significant obstacles to the achievement of certainty in most matters of belief then certainty may no longer seem to be a reasonable goal of inquiry.

This writer and thus this book will opt for the latter understanding of the impact of skepticism on philosophical thought. Certainty in regard to our beliefs, at least in most matters, will be considered un-achievable and the skeptic will, in general, be answered with non-arbitrary beliefs. What is and what is not a non-arbitrary belief needs some spelling out but for now it should suffice to say that this process will be understood, in part, in terms of what works.

Mistaken Beliefs that Work

In a working understanding of belief recommendation there is a need to distinguish between beliefs that work and beliefs that appear to work. If we use what works as part of our criteria for belief justification then beliefs that seem to work would, in effect, become beliefs that are, for all intents and purposes, partly justified. After all, it would seem that if working beliefs are beliefs that are to be recommended, then beliefs that appear to work are beliefs that would appear to be recommended. Since, however, beliefs must be accepted or rejected on the basis of their workability, beliefs that appear to work are beliefs that, in a working system of belief justification, are indistinguishable from beliefs that really work.

An instance and particularly horrid example of this type of problem can be found in a poem transcribed by some Christian monks who recorded a terrible custom of some ancient Irish tribes. The poem goes like this,

> Here used to be
> A high idol with many fights,
> Which was named the Cromm Cruaich;
> It made every tribe to be without peace.
>
> 'T was a sad evil!
> Brave Gaels used to worship it.
> From it they would not without tribute ask
> To be satisfied as to their portion of the hard world.
>
> He was their god,
> The withered Cromm with many mists,
> The people whom he shook over every host,
> The everlasting kingdom they shall not have.
>
> To him without glory
> They would kill their piteous, wretched offspring
> With much wailing and peril,
> To pour their blood around Cromm Cruaich.
>
> Milk and corn
> They would ask from him speedily
> In return for one-third of their healthy issue:
> Great was the horror and scare of him.

The poem continues but this section is sufficient for our purposes. Similar reports of human sacrifice can be found in Julius Caesar's comments on the inhabitants of Britain when Caesar notes that the Celts "make wicker-work images of vast size the limbs of which they fill with living men and set on fire." A possible explanation of the reason and source of these terrible rituals is, as Gilbert Murray notes, the two most important issues for primitive man; the tribe supply and the food supply.

> on what does the collective desire, or collective dread, of the primitive community chiefly concentrate? On two things, the food-supply and the tribe-supply, the desire not to die of famine and not to be harried or conquered by the neighboring tribe. The fertility of the earth and the fertility of the tribe....

Thus, under this hypothesis, the purpose and reason for the human sacrifice by the ancient Irish tribes was to ensure a fertile earth. From our privileged historical position it is easy to claim that it was the efforts in the fields, and not the worship of Cromm, that worked in getting a good crop. But this answer was not available to the early Irish tribes. If they were to use, or did use, the criteria of going with what works to explain the need for sacrifices an advocate of working beliefs might be forced to admit that their beliefs on this matter were partly justified—given the circumstances. That is, while there is probably no god named Cromm, worship and sacrifice to this fictional entity, combined with seeding and planting, might work in the sense that crops are available for harvest.

The problem presented in this example, one might say, is that the early Irish tribes have combined farming with their worship of Cromm. While it might be the case that both Cromm worship and field work are necessary and sufficient for good crops it might also be the case that plowing and seeding, without Cromm worship, is sufficient for good crops. It is not always possible, however, to experiment with one's beliefs and this is especially true if this experiment involves a society's food supply.

Conclusion

The working theory of belief recommendation, by itself, and as an answer to the skeptic, leaves something to be desired. While having beliefs that allow for a predictive, efficient and effective relationship with the cosmos would seem to be of considerable value, this method of investigation would also appear to need supplementation. The next chapter discusses a possible supplement to the working criteria of belief recommendation.

CHAPTER 12

CONSISTENCY, CONTRADICTIONS AND SOME DANGERS OF BEING OVERLY CONSISTENT

Consistency in Thought and Action

A good example of what is intended by the term 'consistency' can be found in a work entitled *The Golden Bough*. *The Golden Bough* is, among many other things, an extensive documentation of the beliefs of many different cultures. In the selection below the author of the book, Sir James Frazer, is discussing a report concerning some of the beliefs of the people of Fiji:

'The custom of voluntary suicide on the part of the old men, which is among their most extraordinary usages, is also connected with their superstitions respecting a future life. They believe that persons enter upon the delights of their Elysium [isle of paradise] with the same faculties, mental and physical, that they possess at the hour of death, in short, that the spiritual life commences where the corporeal existence terminates. With these views, it is natural that they should desire to pass through this change before their mental and bodily powers are so enfeebled by age as to deprive them of their capacity for enjoyment. To this motive must be added the contempt which attaches to physical weakness among a nation of warriors, and the wrongs and insults which await those who are no longer able to protect themselves.

When therefore a man finds his strength declining with the advance of age, and feels he will soon be unequal to discharge the duties of this life, and to partake in the pleasures of that which is to come, he calls together his relations, and tells them that he is now worn out and useless, that he sees they are all ashamed of him and that he has determined to be buried.' So on a day appointed they used to meet and bury him alive....

For the purposes of this work consistency will be defined, in part, in terms of statements. Beliefs, one might say, can be expressed in the form of statements. For instance one could summarize some of the Fijians' beliefs concerning the after-life with the following statements:

1. There is life after death.
2. The next life is, in part, a continuation of this life.
3. As humans age they lose certain desirable faculties.

Believing something like the above to be true the Fijian warriors drew the inference that if they wanted certain faculties in the next life then they had to die while they still possessed these qualities in this life.

Consistency, given the above, can be understood as statements and the relationships that exist between the terms in these statements. A consistent set of terms is a set of terms which, if considered together, fail to contradict each other. Inconsistent sets of words are sets of words that, if considered as a group, yield contradictions. For example, consider the following set of statements:

1. All bachelors are unmarried males.
2. Eric is a bachelor.
3. Eric is an unmarried male.

These three statements are all consistent. It is quite possible that all the above sets of terms could be simultaneously true as none of the sets contradict each other. On the other hand the following set of terms contains a contradiction:

1. All bachelors are unmarried males.
2. Ted is a bachelor.
3. Ted is married to Kathryn.

Ted cannot both be married to Kathryn and still be a bachelor. Ted might be married to Kathryn and behave as if he was a bachelor, but that is not the same thing. In a similar fashion the following set also contains a contradiction:

1. No mammals are warm-blooded.
2. All mammals are warm-blooded.

It is hard to imagine how to make sense out of the above two statements without disregarding one or the other. Statements containing contradictions are thus sets of statements where the meanings of these statements are in conflict; the language is internally 'against itself.' Since one of the purposes of language is to facilitate the flow of information through sets of symbols, when these symbols have conflicting meanings, the flow of information is, at the very least, impeded. Contradictions are thus, in a sense, the antithesis of comprehensible thought and are something one should try to avoid.

Contradictions and Philosophy

Philosophers, in general, are very disturbed by, and distrustful of, beliefs sets that contain contradictions. In a discipline that aims at providing a comprehensible account of experience, statements that muddle and confuse this effort are treated with great suspicion. It is useful, nonetheless, to distinguish between carefully constructed linguistic paradoxes presented in the form of apparent contradictions and pure contradictions. The stimulation of thought through the use of seemingly incongruous statements is different from a pointless confusion of symbols. Logical and linguistic paradoxes are thus not necessarily the same thing as the careless use of language.

Consistency and Working Beliefs, A Quick Introduction

The combination of beliefs that work with beliefs that are consistent provides two criteria by which beliefs can be judged and compared. The criterion of workableness ensures that one's beliefs are, at least in some respects, testable. The criterion of consistency, if nothing else, insures that our thoughts are kept in a somewhat orderly and understandable fashion. Both standards, it would appear, could be of some use in constructing non-arbitrary beliefs about the totality. Non-arbitrary beliefs, while not the same thing as infallible beliefs, are nonetheless beliefs that can seemingly be recommended over arbitrary beliefs. This, one might say, becomes especially true if it is allowed that beliefs are significantly intertwined with our lives and how we choose to live.

CHAPTER 13

SELF-AWARENESS, CONSISTENCY, WORKING BELIEFS AND AN ANSWER TO THE SKEPTIC

A Foundational Philosophy

If Descartes' "I think therefore I am" can be considered to be a self-evident foundation to any who are self-aware then the answer proposed to the skeptic in this work begins with the foundation of self-existence. If the reader, or so the argument goes, is self-aware then the reader can be certain of his or her own existence. We may know nothing else but the experience of perception guarantees that there is something that perceives this perception.

With the knowledge of our self-existence in place we can start to discuss our perceptions and experiences with confidence that these things, at the very least, are perceived and experienced. Without certifiable access to anything beyond our own thoughts it becomes impossible to know, however, if these experiences correspond to anything beyond our-self. It is, nonetheless, still possible to know that we are having perceptions and thoughts. If we further combine our experiences with that which works and a standard of consistency it becomes possible to construct additional and recommendable, but not certain, beliefs.

Beliefs and Cross-Word Puzzles;
Putting It All Together

The crossword puzzle, a metaphor owed directly to Susan Haack, provides a good example of how consistent and workable beliefs can be combined. The puzzle as a whole can be taken to represent the context and nature of our perceptions and our experiences; it is our experience of the totality. The clues in the crossword puzzle can be taken to represent the beliefs that work and the crossing of the words can be seen to represent the need for consistency in our beliefs.

In short, and at the danger of being repetitious, the puzzle is the sum of our experiences in life; it is what is to be explained. The clues to the puzzle are beliefs that work; they are the beliefs that allow for an effective and efficient interaction with our experiences. The crossings of the words represent the requirements of consistency in thought; they represent the need to be coherent in our use of symbols.

Working beliefs, however, it must be remembered have an inherent limitation. Working beliefs do not claim to be true. Working beliefs are not a final or complete account of reality. Working beliefs are merely beliefs that facilitate interaction with that which we experience. Working beliefs do not claim to provide a final or a total description of reality; working beliefs only claim to assist us in inter-acting with what we experience.

Conclusion

If the reader has come away with the impression that a very daunting task lies in front of the thinker the reader is not, in my opinion, over-reacting. A genuine study of these issues is hard and fraught with difficulties. A great deal of very good philosophy starts, however, with the realization that one does not know nearly as much as one thought one knew and that, about the most important matters, one is especially ignorant. Without this acknowledgment of ignorance the quest for wisdom is unlikely to ever seriously begin.

PART III

A FEW FINAL THOUGHTS

A Discussion of Some Related Issues

The final section of this work will take a quick look at some questions and thoughts directly related to the system of belief recommendation just presented. The following is too short to be anything but a beginning of a discussion of some of these matters but that is all that is really possible in this setting.

CHAPTER 14

DISAGREEMENT AND THE GOAL OF INQUIRY

Inquiry into the evidence of a doctrine is not to be made once for all, and then taken as finally settled. It is never lawful to stifle a doubt; for either it can be honestly answered by means of the inquiry already made, or else it proves that the inquiry was not complete.

— W.K. Clifford "The Ethics of Belief"

The Goal of Inquiry

Earlier in the work it was suggested that philosophy, religion and theology shared a common quality of attempting to render an explanation of the totality. Differences exist in how these types of explanations are derived but in many respects a common goal of explanation is sought by these varied attempts at comprehension. Part of the goal of philosophical inquiry then, given the preceding, is an attempt to render an explanation of experience.

If the preceding is reasonably accurate then some interesting considerations seem to suggest themselves. For instance, if Tim experiences (a), (b) and (t) and Susan experiences (a), (b) and (s) then we might well expect Tim and Susan to agree on some points and disagree on other points. If the purpose of inquiry is to explain our experiences, and if our experiences are different, it should not be surprising to discover that our explanations are sometimes different. Indeed if Susan considers (s) relevant in understanding (a) and (b) and Tim considers (t) relevant to understanding (a) and (b) then substantial and legitimate disagreement might well exist between Tim and Susan on even the most basic issues.

Agreeing to Disagree

The situation, in sum, is something like the following. My explanations need to take into account my experiences and perceptions. If one consistently applies this same standard to others who attempt philosophy then one must expect them to derive their explanations, at least in part, from their experiences and perceptions as well. Similarly, it would seem, if one expect beliefs, at least to some degree, to be derived from experiences and perceptions then one must allow for the possibility that those who have different experiences might well have different explanations.

If something like the above is correct then it would seem hard to deny that any individual, when compared to another individual, might have some very different ideas about life and life's issues. Indeed it is hard to discuss the history of any nation or people without discussing the various factions who divide otherwise unified groups. The interpretation and comprehension of experience is, at the very least, a difficult and confusing matter and one should be prepared for disagreement on these matters.

Distress, Pleasure and Philosophy

The chapter opened with a quote from W. K. Clifford's essay "The Ethics of Belief" and I would like to close it with a further citation from this same text. Clifford's essay literally attempts to deal with 'the ethics of belief' and while this is an important issue a full discussion of this matter in this setting is not possible. For the moment I can only hint at some of my thoughts with the following quote from Clifford.

To know all about anything is to know how to deal with it under all circumstances. We feel much happier and more secure when we think we know precisely what to do, no matter what happens, than when we have lost our way and do not know where to turn. And if we have supposed ourselves to know all about anything, and to be capable of doing what is fit in regard to it, we naturally do not like to find that we are really ignorant and powerless, that we have to begin again at the beginning, and try to learn what the thing is and how it is to be dealt with—if indeed anything can be learnt about it. It is the sense of power attached to a sense of knowledge that makes men desirous of believing, and afraid of doubting.

This sense of power is the highest and best of pleasures when the belief on which it is founded is a true belief, and has been fairly earned by investigation. For then we may justly feel that it is common property, and hold good for others as well as for ourselves. Then we may be glad, not that *I* have learned secrets by which I am safer and stronger, but that *we men* have got mastery over more of the world; and we shall be strong, not for ourselves, but in the name of Man and in his strength. But if the belief has been accepted on insufficient evidence, the pleasure is a stolen one.

CHAPTER 15

SOME CONCERNS AND SOME CRITIQUES

Fallibilism

What follows is a short analysis of the system of belief justification that was presented in the second section of this book. A system which for this discussion I will term 'a fallibilistic system,' or 'fallibilism.'

Certainty, Justification and Beliefs

While it might be pointed out that fallibilism does recognize and make reference to at least one foundation, one self-evident foundation, fallibilism does not claim certitude for most of its recommendations. Since, all things being equal, a certain belief is preferable to an uncertain belief it would seem that, all things being equal, a certain philosophy is preferable to a fallibilistic philosophy. While the issue of certainty and philosophy is an interesting point to discuss it is too large a question to delve into at this point in the text. If certainty is considered an un-achievable standard in regard to most of our beliefs then a fallibilistic system of belief recommendation may well seem to be an attractive philosophical alternative. If, on the other hand, certainty is considered an achievable standard in thought, then fallibilistic systems of belief justification will seem too weak to be proper contenders for good philosophical thought.

Self-Evident Foundations

Self-evident foundations, once again, and like all foundations, bring with them a potential difficulty. If a self-evident foundation turns out, in the long run, not to be self-evident then the justification of any belief developed in reference to this foundation can be weakened and sometimes completely compromised. The impact of being forced to re-think a foundation will vary, of course, depending upon the role this foundation had in relation to one's other beliefs.

In the system out-lined in this work the foundation of "I think therefore I am" plays a fairly pivotal role in providing justification for thinking our experiences are real. The loss of the justification for taking experiences seriously would be a loss of the justification for taking working beliefs seriously. The ramifications of the loss of the foundation "I think therefore I am" to fallibilism continue but the above is enough to demonstrate the impact that the loss of foundation can have to a system of thought. All foundational systems suffer from this same malady. Anytime you build on a foundation the risk is incurred that this foundation may prove, upon further examination, to be problematic.

Working Beliefs and Goals

A working belief was defined as a belief that allows for effective and efficient interaction with our experiences and the cosmos. What counts as effective and efficient, given this definition, would seem to be something that could vary depending upon one's goal or purpose. If, for instance, one's goal is to make war upon one's neighbors what works might be very different from what works if one's goal is to establish peaceful relations with these same people. What one wants thus partly determines what one believes and this equation may seem, at first, more than a little troublesome.

While it is admitted that part of what works is defined in terms of goals and desires it must also be remembered that part of what works is also defined via reference to things seemingly beyond our control. Working beliefs are thus not equivalent to wishes and desires. While what is wanted, in part, shapes what works beliefs that work are also shaped by that which must be worked. Working beliefs are thus partly determined by goals but they are also seemingly developed in reference to things other than our wishes and desires.

Ethics, Goals and Working Beliefs

The formation of beliefs via goal based effectiveness tests leads one directly into questions of ethics and values. Not every goal and desire, one might say, is morally equal. A discussion of what is and what is not a morally equal goal is beyond the scope of this work but a very readable work on Western ethical thought is the third edition of James Rachel's *The Elements of Moral Philosophy*. Any one desiring to look further into this matter would be well advised to put this book on their reading list.

APPENDIX

A SHORT LIST OF SOURCES
AND SOME
SUGGESTIONS FOR FURTHER READING

Chapter One: The Norse Gods, Non-Arbitrary Beliefs and "The Truth About Earthquakes"

An excellent book for children and a great source on mythology is *Bulfinch's Mythology*. Many other composites and encyclopedia's of myth exist and are also available. I have a marked preference for illustrated versions of these things and tend to reference both Richard Cavendish's *Mythology an Illustrated Encyclopedia* and Arthur Cottrell's *The Encyclopedia of Mythology*. The story discussed in this chapter can be found, among other places, in the Cottrell work mentioned above under the entry of Sigyn in his section on Norse Mythology.

Thomas Moravec is to be thanked for his comments and suggestions on the thoughts in this chapter.

Bulfinch, Thomas, *Bulfinch's Mythology*, illustrated edition, Crown Publishers, 1979.

Cavendish, Richard, *Mythology An Illustrated Encyclopedia*, Crescent Books, 1987.

Cotterell, Arthur, *The Encyclopedia of Mythology*, Anness Publishing, 1996.

Chapter Two: An American Philosopher and Some Advantages of Science

A good place to read some of Peirce's work directly is H.S. Thayer's *Pragmatism, The Classical Writings*. Reading the full essay discussed in this chapter ("The Fixation of Belief") is recommended. "How to Make Our Ideas Clear" is another excellent paper by Peirce and is another very good place to start studying some of his thought. Both of these papers are in the work by Thayer noted below. The quoted material on page 4 can be found on pages 68-69 of the Thayer text, the short quote on page 5 can be located on page 70 and the quote beginning on page 5 and ending on page 5 can be found on pages 73-74.

Many thanks are owed to Mark Neunder for the comments he has made on earlier versions of this chapter and many other chapters.

Thayer, H.S., *Pragmatism The Classical Writings*, Hackett Publishing, 1982.

Chapter Three: Philosophy, Science and the Totality

A great place to read about Western science and Ancient Greek philosophy is F.M. Cornford's book *Before and After Socrates*. Masterfully written the text begins with the rise of Greek thought before discussing Socrates, Plato and Aristotle in little over a hundred pages. The quote from Cornford at the beginning of the chapter can be found on page 21.

Contemporary American psychology uses the term "object permanence" or the "object concept" to describe the notion that things exist independently of observation. See Guy LeFrancois's text entitled *The Lifespan*, pages 142-143 for a more detailed discussion of this matter.

James Swindler is owed a great deal of thanks for his comments on this chapter and many other chapters. Michael Gayle is also to be thanked for his comments on the thoughts in this chapter.

Cornford, F.M., *Before and After Socrates*, Cambridge University Press, 1932; reprinted 1950, 1960 (twice), 1962 (twice), 1964, 1965, 1966, 1968, 1972, 1974, 1976, 1978, 1979, 1981, 1982, 1983, 1984, 1985, 1986, 1987, 1988, 1990, 1991, 1992, 1993, 1996.

LeFrancois, Guy, R., *The Lifespan*, 5th edition, Wadsworth, 1996.

Chapter Four: Philosophy, Theology, Religion and Bertrand Russell

The Basic Writings of Bertrand Russell is a good place to start reading the works of Russell. Russell is a very readable and a very powerful writer. The quote from Russell's "A Free Man's Worship" in this chapter can be found on pages 66-67 of the same text.

The quote at the beginning of the chapter, from Gilbert Murray, can be found on page 5 of his enchanting little book entitled "Five Stages of Greek Religion."

The definitional distinctions employed in this chapter (e.g. The Foundational Philosopher, The Multiple-Foundational Theologian, etc.) is a style of philosophy and writing that is derived from the work and thought of Susan Haack. Haack's recent books *Evidence and Inquiry* and *Manifesto of Passionate Moderate*, in addition to a number of articles and numerous lectures, have directly shaped and greatly influenced the discussions in this text. Some of the best work, in this writer's opinion, in modern and contemporary philosophy is to be found in Haack's publications. The works and articles mentioned above will be discussed in more detail in the notes to chapters eight, ten, twelve, thirteen and fifteen.

Lucas Niiller is owed special thanks for his very helpful suggestions on the definitions offered and discussed in this chapter and for his editorial efforts on an early draft of this text.

Haack, Susan, *Evidence and Inquiry*, Blackwell, 1993, reprinted in
    1994, 1995 (twice), 1996 (twice), 1997, 1998.
Haack, Susan, *Manifesto of a Passionate Moderate*, University of
    Chicago Press, 1998.
Murray, Gilbert, *Five Stages of Greek Religion*, Watts and Co.,
    1935, 1943, 1946.
Russell, Bertrand, *The Basic Writings of Bertrand Russell*, edited
    by Robert Egner and Lester Denonn, A Touchstone/Simon and
    Schuster publication, 1961.

Chapter Five: The Buddha, Poisoned Arrows and The Four Noble Truths

A very good book on religion is Huston Smith's *The World's
Religions*. Smith's work is both very knowledgeable and very
readable. The chapter on Christianity, I would argue, is a little
partial to this same system but this should not deter anyone from
taking a look at this book. The quoted material from the Buddha at
the beginning of the chapter can be found in *The World's Religions*
on pages 95-96 and quote concerning the third noble truth can be
found on page 103 of the same text.

The discussion of Buddhism in this chapter is drawn from the
afore mentioned text, William Young's *The World's Religions;
World Views and Contemporary Issues*, Ed. Milller's *Questions
That Matter* and Friedhelm Hardy's *The World's Religions; The
Religions of Asia*. The list of eight-fold path is taken directly from
Miller's *Questions That Matter* and can be located on page 273.

Hardy, Friedhelm, *The World's Religions: The Religions of Asia*,
    Routledge London, published as part of *The World Religions*
    in 1988 and reprinted in 1990.
Miller, Ed., *Questions That Matter, An Invitation to Philosophy*,
    shorter edition, McGraw-Hill Inc., 1984, 1987, 1992, 1993.
Smith, Huston, *The World's Religions: Our Great Wisdom Tradi-
    tions*, HarperCollins, 1991. (First published under the title *The
    Religions of Man* in 1958.)

Young, William, A., *The World's Religions, Worldviews and Contemporary Issues*, Prentice Hall, 1995.

Chapter Six: Divine Foundations and a Necessary God?

It is possible to find some very good treatments of the divine foundation discussed in this chapter. Michael Martin, in his work *Atheism, A Philosophical Justification*, provides a good summary and a good critique of this issue. Both John Hick and Baruch Brody, in the works listed below, supply the beginning student with a number of discussions centered directly on this question.

Brody, Baruch, *Readings in the Philosophy of Religion, An Analytic Approach*, Prentice-Hall, 1974.

Hick, John, *Classical and Contemporary Readings in the Philosophy of Religion*, Prentice Hall, 1964, 1970, 1990.

Martin, Michael, *Atheism, A Philosophical Justification*, Temple University Press, 1990.

Chapter Seven: Personal Finance, Appearance and Reality

Shel Silverstein's *Where the Sidewalk Ends* and *The Missing Piece Meets the Big "O"* are both simply wonderful books. While no use is made of the latter text in this work it is well worth the time to find and read. The poem "Smart" can be found in *Where the Sidewalk Ends* on page 35. The quoted material from Santayana at the beginning of the chapter can be found on page 1 on his work *Skepticism and Animal Faith*.

Santayana, George, *Scepticism and Animal Faith*, Dover Publications, 1923; reprint in 1955.

Silverstein, Shel, *The Missing Piece Meets the Big "O*," Harpercollins, 1981

Silverstein, Shel, *Where the Sidewalk Ends: The Poems and Drawings of Shel Silverstein*, Harpercollins, 1974.

Chapter Eight: The Thinker, The Skeptic and a French Philosopher

The definition of skepticism found at the beginning of the chapter is drawn from Peter Angeles' *Dictionary of Philosophy* and can be found on page 258.

Meditations on First Philosophy is a good place to start reading the works of Rene Descartes. Of Descartes' writings it is this effort for which he is seemingly most remembered. The translations of Descartes in this chapter were taken from *Descartes Selected Philosophical Writings,* pages 76-80, with the exception of the last quote which was drawn from Castell, Bochert and Zucker's *An Introduction to Modern Philosophy,* page 30.

The answer to the skeptic that is suggested and discussed in this text derives directly from the work and thoughts of Susan Haack. Excellent discussions of this program are available from the author herself and in particular I would point the reader to her text *Evidence and Inquiry* and her paper "A Foundherentist Theory of Empirical Justification" for detailed expositions of these matters.

Angeles, Peter, *Dictionary of Philosophy*, Barnes and Noble Books, 1981.

Castell, Borchert, Zucker, *An Introduction to Modern Philosophy; Examining the Human Condition*, MacMillan College Publishing, 1943, 1963, 1976, 1983, 1988, 1994, 6th edition.

Descartes, Rene, *Meditations on First Philosophy*, translated and introduced by Lafleur, Laurence, J., MacMillan Publishing, thirty-first printing, 1989.

Descartes; *Selected Philosophical Writings*, translated by John Cottingham, Robert Stoothoff and Dugald Murdoch with an introduction by John Cottingham, Cambridge University Press, 1988, 1989.

Haack, Susan, *Evidence and Inquiry*, Blackwell, 1993, reprinted in 1994, 1995, 1996, 1997, 1998.

Haack, Susan, *Manifesto of a Passionate Moderate*, University of Chicago Press, 1998.

Haack, Susan, "A Foundherentist Theory of Empirical Justification," appearing in *Theory of Knowledge: Classic and Contemporary Sources*, edited by Pojman, L., 2nd edition, Wadsworth 1998. Reprinted in E. Sosa's and J. Kim's *Epistemology*, Blackwell 1999.

Haack, Susan, "American Pragmatism," to appear in Danish in *Videnskab og Sprog, (Science and Language)*, edited by Paul Lubike, Politikens Press, Copenhagen.

Haack, Susan, ""We Pragmatists...." Peirce and Rorty in Conversation," *Partisan Review*, PR/1, 1997. Reprinted in *Manifesto of a Passionate Moderate*, University of Chicago Press, 1998.

Chapter Nine: Parrots, Invalid Kings and a German Philosopher

A Thousand and One Arabian Nights is simply a great pleasure to read. Of Francis Bacon's three classes of books (those that are to be digested, those that are to be tasted and those that are to be swallowed) it is one that is to be swallowed. The story of the husband and parrot can be found on pages 49-50.

Kant's discussion of perceived and the unperceived can be found in his work *The Critique of Pure Reason*. This text is one of the most difficult reads in modern philosophy and it is *not* recommended until the beginning student of philosophy is comfortable reading less difficult works. Kant is best approached via commentators and Will Durant's *The Story of Philosophy* is a good place to start reading a commentary on Kant and the other great Western philosophers. *Sophie's World* by Jostein Gaarder is another excellent introduction to the history of western thought. W.T. Jones's *A History of Western Philosophy, Volumes 1-5* is another very good starting point for a study of Western thought and Western philosophers.

Durant, Will, *The Story of Philosophy*, A Washington Square
  Publication of Pocket Books, 1926, 1927, 1933, 1954, 1955
  and 1961.
Gaarder, Jostein, *Sophie's World*, Berkley Books, 1991, 1994,
  1996.
Jones, W.T., *A History of Western Philosophy*, in five volumes,
  Harcourt Brace Javnovich College Publishers, 1952, 1970 and
  1980.
Kant, Immanuel, *Critique of Pure Reason*, translated by Norman
  Kemp Smith, unabridged edition, St. Martins Press, 1929,
  1965.
Zipes, Jack, *Arabian Nights, The Marvels and Wonders of The
  Thousand and One Nights*, Penguin Books, 1991.

Chapter Ten: Pumpkins, Shade Trees and Other Considerations in Agriculture

The working standard of truth introduced in this chapter
derives, in part, from the pragmatic philosophical tradition begun
by Charles Peirce and carried on by William James, John Dewey,
George Mead, Ferdinand Schiller and C.I. Lewis.

The working standard of truth discussed in this chapter derives
also, in part, from Susan Haack's graduate lectures at the
University of Miami (1990-1992), her work *Evidence and Inquiry*
and her papers "American Pragmatism," "We Pragmatists....Peirce
and Rorty in Conversation" and "A Foundherentist Theory of
Empirical Justification." I owe the above list of the classical
pragmatists to Susan Haack's paper "American Pragmatism"

The discussions of infallibility and goal driven epistemologies
are heavily influenced by Haack work's *Evidence and Inquiry* and
her paper "American Pragmatism."

The story by Mark Twain, "How I Edited an Agricultural
Paper" can be found in *The Complete Short Stories of Mark Twain*
edited by Charles Neider on pages 45-8. Another very good work
by Twain is his *Letters From The Earth*. The reader should be

warned, however, that this last text by Twain is heavily critical of what might be termed traditional or institutional Christianity.

Haack, Susan, *Evidence and Inquiry*, Blackwell, 1993, reprinted in 1994, 1995, 1996, 1997, 1998.

Haack, Susan, *Manifesto of a Passionate Moderate*, University of Chicago Press, 1998.

Haack, Susan, "American Pragmatism," to appear in Danish in *Videnskab og Sprog*, (*Science and Language*), edited by Paul Lubike, Politikens Press, Copenhagen.

Haack, Susan, "We Pragmatists...." Peirce and Rorty in Coversation," *Partisan Review*, PR/1, 1997. Reprinted in *Manifesto of a Passionate Moderate*, University of Chicago Press, 1998.

Haack, Susan, "A Foundherentist Theory of Empirical Justification," appearing in *Theory of Knowledge: Classic and Contemporary Sources*, edited by Pojman, L., 2nd edition, Wadsworth 1998. Reprinted in E. Sosa's and J. Kim's *Epistemology*, Blackwell 1999.

Twain, Mark, *Letters From the Earth*, edited by Bernard DeVoto, HarperPerennial of Harper Collins, 1938, 1942, 1944, 1946, 1959, 1962, 1991.

Twain, Mark, *The Complete Short Stories of Mark Twain*, edited by Charles Neider, Bantam Books, 1981, eight printings through 1990.

Chapter Eleven: Beliefs that Work, Mistaken Beliefs that Work and an Old Irish God

The poem in this chapter is taken from *Celtic Myth and Legend* by Charles Squire. It can be located on pages 38-39 of the same work. The quote from Gilbert Murray is drawn from his wonderful little book entitled *The Five Stages of Greek Religion* and can be found on page 29.

Haack, Susan, *Evidence and Inquiry*, Blackwell, 1993, reprinted in 1994, 1995, 1996, 1997, 1998.

Haack, Susan, *Manifesto of a Passionate Moderate*, University of Chicago Press, 1998.

Haack, Susan, "American Pragmatism," to appear in Danish in *Videnskab og Sprog*, (*Science and Language*), edited by Paul Lubike, Politikens Press, Copenhagen.

Haack, Susan, ""'We Pragmatists...." Peirce and Rorty in Coversation." *Partisan Review*, PR/1, 1997. Reprinted in *Manifesto of a Passionate Moderate*, University of Chicago Press, 1998.

Haack, Susan, "A Foundherentist Theory of Empirical Justification" appearing in *Theory of Knowledge: Classic and Contemporary Sources*, edited by Pojman, L., 2nd edition, Wadsworth 1998. Reprinted in E. Sosa's and J. Kim's *Epistemology*, Blackwell 1999.

Murray, Gilbert, *The Five Stages of Greek Religion*, Watts and CO., 1935, 1943, 1946.

Squire, Charles, *Celtic Myth and Legend*, Newcastle Publishing, 1987.

Chapter Twelve: Consistency, Contradictions and Some Dangers of Being Overly Consistent

The standard of consistency in thought is a standard that has been part of Western philosophical thought from at least the times of Ancient Greece. The combination of consistency and working beliefs into a standard for belief justification is derived directly from chapters one and four of Susan Haack's *Evidence and Inquiry*, her graduate lectures at the University of Miami (1990-1992) and her paper "A Foundherentist Account of Empirical Justification."

The quote from *The Golden Bough* can be found on page 230.

Frazer, James, George, *The Golden Bough*, an abridgement from the second and third editions, edited and introduced by Robert Fraser, Oxford University Press, 1994.

Haack, Susan, *Evidence and Inquiry*, Blackwell, 1993, reprinted in 1994, 1995, 1996. 1997, 1998.

Haack, Susan, "A Foundherentist Theory of Empirical Justification" appearing in *Theory of Knowledge: Classic and Contemporary Sources*, edited by Pojman, L., 2nd edition, Wadsworth 1998. Reprinted in E. Sosa's and J. Kim's *Epistemology*, Blackwell, 1999.

Chapter Thirteen: Self-Awareness, Consistency, Working Beliefs and an Answer to the Skeptic

The notes and accreditations appearing in chapter twelve, with the exception of the first sentence, apply equally to the material in chapter twelve. The metaphor/concept of the cross-word puzzle is taken directly from Haack's *Evidence and Inquiry* and her essay "A Foundherentist Account of Empirical Justification."

The definition of wisdom as "knowing that you know nothing" derives from Socrates through the pen of Plato. G.M.A. Grube's *The Trial and Death of Socrates* is a great place to start reading about Socrates.

Grube, G.M.A., *The Trial and Death of Socrates*, a collection of early Platonic essays translated by Grube, Hackett Publishing, 2nd edition, ninth printing, 1987.

Haack, Susan, *Evidence and Inquiry*, Blackwell, 1993, reprinted in 1994, 1995, 1996, 1997, 1998.

Haack, Susan, "A Foundherentist Theory of Empirical Justification" appearing in *Theory of Knowledge: Classic and Contemporary Sources*, edited by Pojman, L., 2nd edition, Wadsworth 1998. Reprinted in E. Sosa's and J. Kim's *Epistemology*, Blackwell, 1999.

Chapter Fourteen: Disagreement and the Goal of Inquiry

Both of the quotes from Clifford in this chapter are drawn from his essay "The Ethics of Belief." Readers who take a look at Clifford's essay might also be interested in readings William James's paper "The Will to Believe." James's paper can be found in H.S. Thayer's, *Pragmatism The Classical Writings* and Clifford's essay can be found in *The Ethics of Belief and Other Essays* pages 70-96.

Clifford, W.K., "The Ethics of Belief," first published in 1877, appearing in *The Ethics of Belief and Other Essays*, Watts and Company, 1947.

Thayer, H.S., *Pragmatism, The Classical Writings*, Hackett Publishing, 1982.

Chapter Fifteen: Some Concerns and Some Critiques

Additional discussions of certainty, problems with certainty and goal referencing epistemologies can be found in Susan Haack's *Evidence and Inquiry, Manifesto of a Passionate Moderate* and her papers "American Pragmatism" and "A Foundherentist Theory of Empirical Justification." The discussions in this chapter stem directly from Haack's work on these matters.

Haack, Susan, *Evidence and Inquiry*, Blackwell, 1993, reprinted in 1994, 1995, 1996. 1997, 1998.

Haack, Susan, *Manifesto of a Passionate Moderate*, University of Chicago Press, 1998.

Haack, Susan, "American Pragmatism," to appear in Danish in *Videnskab og Sprog*, (*Science and Language*), edited by Paul Lubike, Politikens Press, Copenhagen.

Haack, Susan, "A Foundherentist Theory of Empirical Justification" appearing in *Theory of Knowledge: Classic and Contemporary Sources*, edited by Pojman, L., 2nd edition,

Wadsworth 1998. Reprinted in E. Sosa's and J. Kim's *Epistemology*, Blackwell 1999.

Rachels, James, *The Elements of Moral Philosophy*, McGraw-Hill College, third edition 1999, previous editions in 1986 and 1993.

INDEX